Where Will I Live?

Rosemary McCarney

Second Story Press

Croatia

Sometimes scary things happen to good people.

Hungary

When soldiers fight or danger comes

Rwanda

families must pack their things
and search for a safe place to live.

They ride…

Iraq

or walk…

Hungary

or run, hoping to find a peaceful place.

Hungary

But where will *I* live?
Will it be down this road…

Jordan

beyond this hill…

Slovenia

past this fence...

across this sea?

South Sudan

Will I live under a carpet…

Lebanon

beneath some stairs…

Greece

in a tent...

or a whole city of tents?

Kenya

Will where I live be hot and dry?

Lebanon

Cold and wintry?

Cameroon

Will I find one special buddy…

or lots of friends where I live?

Will I be able to sleep in the same place every night?

Lebanon

Will my new bed be just for me?
Or will I still have to share it?

Jordan

So many questions. So many hopes.

Myanmar

After such a long journey, and such a long wait,

Niger

I hope someone smiles and says "Welcome home."
I hope that someone is you.

Library and Archives Canada Cataloguing in Publication

McCarney, Rosemary A., author
Where will I live? / Rosemary McCarney

ISBN 978-1-77260-028-5 (hardback)
ISBN 978-1-77260-044-5 (paperback)

1. Refugee children—Juvenile literature. 2. Refugee children—
Pictorial works. I. Title.

HV640.M29 2017   j362.87   C2016-906761-0

Special thanks to Kathryn Cole for her extraordinary work on this book.

Second Story Press gratefully acknowledges the support of the Ontario Arts Council and the Canada Council for the Arts for our publishing program. We acknowledge the financial support of the Government of Canada through the Canada Book Fund.

Printed and bound in China

ONTARIO ARTS COUNCIL
CONSEIL DES ARTS DE L'ONTARIO
an Ontario government agency
un organisme du gouvernement de l'Ontario

Canada Council   Conseil des Arts
for the Arts   du Canada

Funded by the Government of Canada
Financé par le gouvernement du Canada | Canada

Published by
Second Story Press
20 Maud Street, Suite 401
Toronto, Ontario, Canada
M5V 2M5
www.secondstorypress.ca

Photo Credits

The photos were generously provided by the United Nations High Commission for Refugees from their rich and vast library of images depicting their work around the world on behalf of refugees.

Cover: (front) © UNHCR/Sebastian Rich
(back) © UNHCR/Kate Holt, © UNHCR/
Ivor Prickett, © UNHCR/Phil Behan
Page 2: © UNHCR/Mark Henley
Page 3: © UNHCR/Mark Henley
Page 4: © UNHCR/Kate Holt
Page 5: © UNHCR/Andrew McConnell
Page 6: © UNHCR/Shawn Baldwin
Page 7: © UNHCR/Mark Henley
Page 8: © UNHCR/Mark Henley
Page 9: © UNHCR/J. Kohler
Page 10: © UNHCR/Mark Henley
Page 11: © UNHCR/Ivor Prickett
Page 12: © UNHCR/Sebastian Rich
Page 13: © UNHCR/Ivor Prickett
Page 14: © UNHCR/Aikaterini Kitidi
Page 15: © UNHCR/Shawn Baldwin
Page 16: © UNHCR/Assadullah Nasrullah
Page 17: © UNHCR/Andrew McConnell
Page 18: © UNHCR/Olivier Laban-Mattei
Page 19: © UNHCR/Shawn Baldwin
Page 20: © UNHCR/Mark Henley
Page 21: © UNHCR/Lynsey Addario
Page 22: © UNHCR/Sebastian Rich
Page 23: © UNHCR/Phil Behan
Page 24: © UNHCR/Harandane Dicko